Grief Is Love

Grief Is Love

Inspired by Six Saints and Three Angels

JJ Flowers

Lantern Publishing & Media • Brooklyn, NY

2021
Lantern Publishing & Media
128 Second Place
Brooklyn, NY 11231
www.lanternpm.org

Printed in the United States of America

Library of Congress Cataloging-in-Publication Data

Names: Flowers, J. J., author.
Title: Grief is love / JJ Flowers.
Description: Brooklyn : Lantern Publishing & Media, 2021.
Identifiers: LCCN 2021001304 (print) | LCCN 2021001305 (ebook) | ISBN
   9781590566411 (paperback) | ISBN 9781590566428 (epub)
Subjects: LCSH: Grief. | Separation (Psychology) | Love.
Classification: LCC BF575.G7 F66 2021 (print) | LCC BF575.G7 (ebook) | DDC
   152.4—dc23
LC record available at https://lccn.loc.gov/2021001304
LC ebook record available at https://lccn.loc.gov/2021001305

This book is dedicated to John and Jonpaul, the two brightest lights in my life.
And to everyone who has lost a loved one.
These words are inspired by the Six Saints and Three Angels: May your light see us home.

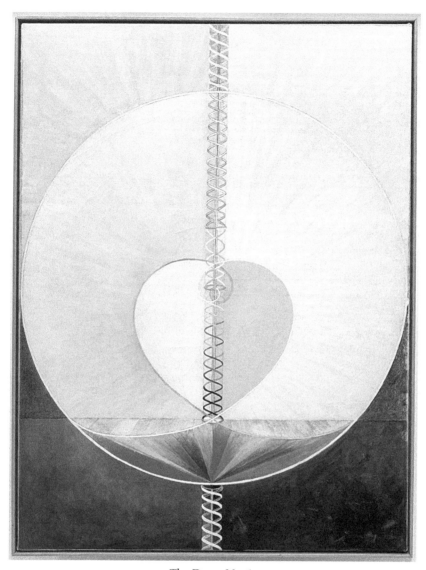

The Dove, No. 1

"I know who you are in truth. I know what you are in truth.
I know how you serve in truth.
You are free, you are free, you are free.
You are love, you are love, you are love."

—**The Book of Love and Creation**

CONTENTS

Hilma af Klint Art and *Grief Is Love*

The Swan, No. 12

I first became aware of Hilma af Klint's pictures in a *New Yorker* article by the gifted art critic Peter Schjeldahl. The article displayed just a few of these masterpieces, but this was enough to alert me to the phenomena. The Guggenheim Museum was holding a show of eighty of Hilma af Klint's paintings. I not only had to see this exhibit, but I had to experience them with *the* Alicia Power.

Alicia Power is a famous spiritualist and, to many, the most gifted energy healer on the planet. She channels the highest-level Creator Beings. To the unfamiliar and the skeptic, this sounds fabulous, I know, but it is true, nonetheless. Alicia is also a dear friend. She enthusiastically agreed to meet me in Manhattan; the travel arrangements were made to travel from her home in Australia, and the date was set.

We walked arm in arm through the doors of the museum into a powerful energy shift brought about by the collection of Hilma's paintings in the gorgeous setting. Surrounded by the Temple Paintings, we first stood there stunned and overwhelmed by the celebration of humanity's place in the spiritual realm; the beauty and joy—and most of all, the spiritual energy—radiating from these large and magnificent works.

Here was a very high light indeed.

Then, even more magic: Hilma zoomed in, and Alicia was in direct communication with her, right there in the museum. She began explaining the symbolism and sacred geometry in her pictures, which Alicia conveyed to me. As we moved up through the spiraling gallery, a crowd occasionally gathered around us, as Alicia pointed out the deeper meaning of the extraordinary art before us. People began weeping, dazed by the connection to Spirit brought by these paintings. In a life filled with art, the Guggenheim exhibit of Hilma af Klint's work became one of the most moving experiences of my lifetime.

Finally, at the end of the day, I found myself seated on a bench in front of some of the paintings. All of a sudden, the energetic power of love began cascading over me; love as an energy . . . love as God source. It was coming from one of the pictures. Tears blurred my vision as I realized the very word *love*, like a wink and a kiss from Hilma herself, emerged from the abstract lines and forms of one of the paintings.

Thank you, Hilma, for creating a canvas that has the awesome power to connect us to the spiritual; the foundation of a meaningful life. At the highest level, grief becomes a gift, like Hilma's paintings, that opens this door. It shows you that you are an incarnate soul who came from the spiritual realm. You arrived in the material realm with an intention; one so often lost in the noise and bustle of our modern lives, but always waiting to be rediscovered. Our human purpose is driven by the universal desire to amplify the energetic power of love and then to use this light to walk each other home.

Just like Hilma af Klint's paintings.

GRIEF IS LOVE

De tio största, No. 2 Barnaaldern

Grief is a story of love.

It has a beginning, a middle, and an end. The end is always heartbreaking; sometimes tragic and often as poignant and beautiful as a sunset. In the best stories, this is delivered with a previously unknown intensity of feeling.

Every love story ends in grief. It is the price we pay for it; for our love. We bought the ending the moment we fell in love.

Grief then becomes the reverberation of love's music into the rest of our lives.

Stories of love are sacred. Grief is sacred. It is not a thing to "get through." It is not a mere pause, and certainly not a "bump" on the otherwise happy road of your life. It is infinitely bigger than that.

Grief arrives as a teacher bearing gifts. It has things to show you. Grief, you will learn, changes as it transforms you one day to the next, one month to the next, one year to the next. It keeps shapeshifting, sometimes dramatically, as you learn its lessons, but . . . it will never go away.

Because your love is forever, grief is forever.

The first thing you need to know about your grief is that love created its every characteristic, especially its size and shape. Since no one else experienced your love story, this exclusivity means no one will ever know what you are going through. You might spend the rest of your life writing about it, painting pictures of it, singing songs about your love and its loss, and still, no one can know your love in the same way you do.

You are walking alone on your grief's path.

This book is my attempt to show up, take your hand, and say, "Come this way, look there, see the light?"

The Tsunami

You are standing on the shore, staring up at a tsunami rising over you and rushing upon you. You are not prepared. No one is ever prepared, even if you were warned it was coming. After the initial bang of shock, you experience a bewildering and intense wave of panic and disbelief, characterized by the words: I can't believe this is happening, I can't believe this happened. . . .

You have lost your loved one.

Grief first arrives as a physical presence. It seizes your body and takes up residence. Its purpose is to wreak havoc. Your life has just changed dramatically, and grief wants you to know it.

The physical expression of grief is different for everyone. Some of its manifestations arrive in a whisper, others land like a blow. Some are fleeting and reoccurring, others never leave. You may get one, some, or all of these symptoms. The ingredients here, their potency and duration, are based on your physical, emotional, and spiritual needs.

It is an original recipe designed for you.

Your grief delivers exactly what you need.

THE BEGINNING

The beginning of grief is overwhelming. Everything must stop as you attempt to absorb what has happened, which is impossible. You cannot fathom the magnitude of your loss. There is little to no comprehension at first.

You will know tears. Tears of grief fall along a wide-ranging spectrum—droplets sliding slowly over cheeks to blinding waterworks accompanied by inhuman cries, breathlessness, convulsive breathing, even spasms. There are long periods when you cannot stop weeping; not to save your life. In the tumultuous first throes of grief, if you are not actually producing tears, you are struggling valiantly to hold them back. Chances are that you will come to know the full range of grief's tearful upheaval.

During this period, you might find yourself googling, "Can crying cause dehydration?" The answer is yes. You wake from sleep to find your pillow wet because you are crying as you sleep. You take to wearing sunglasses at all times.

You soon stumble upon firsts, which trigger more crying: the first night alone; the first morning without your loved one; the first Sunday; the first holiday, birthday, anniversary. Firsts will keep presenting themselves for years to come. Some brush you gently against your loved one's absence, others knock you to your knees in renewed mourning.

Like a wounded bird, you are vulnerable. This defenselessness serves an important purpose. You become at once more sensitive.

This heightened awareness alters your perceptions. Everything seems different—it is different. You have awakened to a changed world.

The Absence

At times your sorrow feels unbearable. Then grief has you alternating between dramatic bouts of crying and a pervasive numbness that consumes mind, body, and soul. The numbness provides a brief respite and gives you a temporary rest. As soon as your strength recovers, you start crying again.

After the initial cataclysm, you retreat to a bedroom or familiar chair, where you sink into a stupor of unfamiliar lethargy. You stare blankly out windows or at walls. A cognitive fog engulfs you. You don't remember things. It is impossible to concentrate. The smallest action is out of the question; it is asking entirely too much.

You are a house that has locked all the doors and barricaded the windows. You simply cannot begin to imagine life without your loved one; you do not try. Your grief is too big to know right now.

You are certain it will break you.

The idea—often without conscious awareness—is that as long as you hold yourself still and unresponsive, no feeling will penetrate your shattered consciousness. Sometimes this numbness arrives less as immobility and more as an absence of feeling, as if your heart made a bargain with your head: If I don't feel anything, I won't have to experience my loss.

Wear this shell like the protective armor it is.

Ignore demands for as long as you need, as long as you can.

At some point, the world will beckon, and you will find yourself responding. You must make your way into the shower, get dressed, drink or eat something. Even though you feel—*so strangely* —as if you are maneuvering through water in slow motion, you adopt the advice given to all people suffering from trauma: Simply place one foot in front of the other. This is how you move forward.

Take comfort in realizing the familiar chair will always be there.

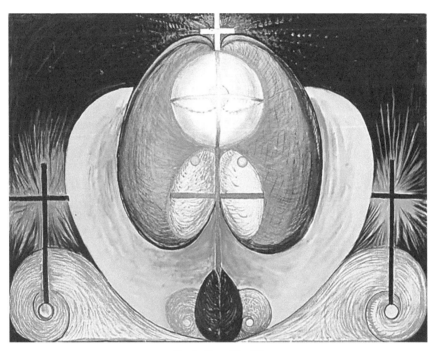

Evolution, No. 10

GREAT CHANGES ARE UPON US

Your grief has arrived in a time of great uncertainty and social upheaval. This even seems like an understatement; the chaos of life on this planet has reached such a feverish pitch. Losing a loved one during this time adds a much deeper layer of insecurity to the feeling that the world is spinning out of control.

This is less an illusion than a given. The sense of being carried along on a swift-moving river of history has been true throughout our human existence. The world has been in constant motion from the beginning. Everything you see is moving—from the molecules in iron to the air in your next breath, all things are a swirling collection of fast-moving particles. Like the cosmos itself, nothing is ever static, and your grief least of all.

A supreme shapeshifter, grief will continue to change you in the days, months, years, and decades ahead, regardless of how the world changes. These shifts can be cataclysmic; an explosive force propelling you into an unforeseen landscape. It can be like a heavy silk robe; a burden of sadness you carry with grace. It can be anything in between.

Your grief showed up during a time of great upheaval; it could be no other way.

Love Knocks at the Door

People often say that time is grief's antidote, but you will discover love is grief's tonic.

The first hint of this comes when, upon news of your loss, love arrives in the support of family and friends. You need this now more than you ever will. Your tears manifest most easily when you confront heartfelt sympathy in others. This is no accident either. It points you in the right direction, sending you into the arms of those who love you.

People call, write, show up on your doorstep. Their faces are full of concern, worry, their own sadness. They often arrive bearing gifts of comfort: food, drink, flowers, themselves. They press poems and prayers into your hands. They want so very much to help you.

Sometimes too, you might notice, these gifts are crazily inappropriate: a flower from your own garden, an unappetizing casserole, a pamphlet from a different church, or a pointless or banal suggestion: *You will survive this . . . It's for the best . . . Things will look better later. . . .*

They do not understand, you think. This is true but does not matter. See them, even these clumsy words, for the acts of concern they are. You might not feel like receiving people and their gifts, but do it anyway. Open your door. Let everyone in. Fall into outstretched arms. Wet everyone's shoulders with your tears.

Let people hold you up in love.

ALCHEMY

For a long time, your vantage point is limited. The cognitive fog, the weight of your tears, the altered light of your future all inhibit comprehension and understanding of the shape life will take without your loved one. Do not try to figure anything out now. You don't have to.

As grief is all consuming, you need only experience your sadness.

At some point, you might imagine the weeping period has abated. You think it is time to attempt something normal: maybe grocery shopping. Yet, as the cashier explains why tomatoes are so expensive, you are terrified to realize she might be speaking Sanskrit for all you can comprehend. Your inability to participate in "normal" life startles you. You try to stop it, the cascade of emotion this understanding brings, but you can't. There you are, staring at the alarmed face of the cashier, blinded by new tears.

You marvel anytime grief is not all consuming. This doesn't happen in the beginning, but as time goes on, there will be whole minutes where you are normal. Normal surprises you, but then, just as quickly, the realization acts like a magnet for grief, and it returns in force, as if to make up for its brief absence.

This is because, in the beginning, any minute not in deep mourning is often experienced as a betrayal of your loved one. How can you feel anything approximating "ordinary" when they no longer walk the earth? When life as you know it is over and here you stand in a strange new world? Your tears reunite you with the loss of your loved one, and grief rushes back to overwhelm any feeling of normal. You are not ready for it. You are unsure you will ever be ready for it.

Still, grief continues working its alchemy.

You might be taking on an innocuous task, like sorting the pile of mail that awaits you. Bills and advertisements are mixed in with condolence cards. You dig in, going through the pile, but suddenly find yourself staring in dumbfounded wonder at the trite image on a sympathy card: the sun streaming through clouds over the ocean. Tears suddenly fill your eyes. You cannot understand how anything can be so beautiful.

Love, you see, has busted your heart wide open.

Operating with a Broken Heart

How long does the intense longing and sadness last? As long as you are able to experience your loved one in their absence. For some the light does indeed diminish over time, but it never disappears altogether. For many of us, the connection to our loved one is more precious than our next breath, and we keep it close forever.

This is the purpose of your grief, to maintain the connection to your loved one.

Grief respects no timeline. It almost always lasts longer than what other people think it should. These are people who don't understand, who, in fact, don't have a clue. Any certitude about grief's arrival or departure date is foolish, plain and simple. Like guessing the number of grains of sand on a beach, you could be right—but it is unlikely.

While your grief begins to weave its purpose into the fabric of your being, your sorrow continues to act as a great weight. Sometimes, to even speak of it feels like a violation. Your grief cannot fit in words. You do not try.

Some people mistake this for depression, as it still feels as if you are moving through water and the simplest tasks continue to require Herculean effort. Grief, however, is not depression; it is the embodiment—heart, mind, and soul—of the loss of your love.

Broken hearts have never won marathons.

Other emotions are amplified during this period as well, including a feeling of separation. You feel isolated and alone in your grief.

It is a solitary journey. Again, nothing in life is as personal as losing your loved one.

It is common to attempt to mitigate grief with too much alcohol, drugs, or overeating, but these only serve to separate you from your grief and the intensity of your feelings. Anything that deadens or numbs your response to grief works against you and acts as fuel for the negative, magnifying and enlarging it, and adding unwelcome additions to your grief: bitterness, anger, hopelessness, and despair.

Similarly, TV first appears as a balm to your strained senses. You can forget your missing loved one, your changed world, and your altered circumstances for long interludes of time. You become lost in the endless stream of imaginary worlds. Sometimes we need this respite, but too much TV has a pernicious effect. It steals your heightened sensitivity and begins to separate you from the poignancy of your loss.

Your grief, you will learn, is the velvet bridge to your loved one.

Here is a picture of your future grief, years or even decades from now: There will be times, often unexpected and seemingly random, where your loved one appears so vividly in your mind as to be present. It will fill you with the same powerful longing and desire you feel now, only later you experience this as their love washing over you in a previously unknown poignancy and beauty.

Your grief is building this connection now.

The one activity that helps (everything) the most during this time is walking. Step outside. Aim for the nearest park or wilderness area. Breathe deeply as you walk. Move slowly. Instead of thinking, look for the simple beauty that surrounds you in nature: clouds decorating the bowl of sky; the green reach of mature trees; the noisy finches who live there; a neighbor's rain-washed flower garden.

If troubled thoughts emerge, return to the simple offerings of nature.

Walking is a healing exercise.

Then rest. Sleep. Dream of your loved one. As much as you can and as long you need too. Without waking awareness, things are happening during rest and sleep. Your consciousness is adjusting to the new world.

It is finding the best way for you to move forward.

Remembrance

All religions and cultures have ceremonies that mark the end of life. These come at the earliest stages of your grief; you will not feel ready for it. Despite this, of course you will have to attend to your loved one's burial or cremation, funeral or memorial. This, too, is not an accident. These ceremonies serve to connect us and our loss to the love carried in our wider community.

The planning and organizing of the funeral or memorial can challenge the best of us in normal times, and normal left the day your loved one died. For the bereaved, the funeral is always overwhelming. Doing anything is difficult—it feels impossible. There is no way around this.

Reach out to others; allow family members and friends to help you.

If you and your loved one belong to a religion, you will likely have a more traditional funeral. In the not-too-distant past, funerals were sober affairs that emphasized the end of life, the loss of the departed, and transcendent hope. Memorials that celebrate a life well lived, which are now becoming more popular, are finally altering even the most somber, traditional funerals, and in recent times, there has been a blurring of funerals and memorials.

Like poetry, funerals say the most with the least; the simpler and shorter the better. Ostentatious and elaborate funerals detract from what is meaningful in your loved one's life and indeed what is sacred in their passing. Less extravagant and more modest ceremonies invite to the gathering what is consequential and profound.

If your loved one is cremated and the ashes are not to be buried in a cemetery, you choose between keeping them and dispensing them. If you keep them, you will need a special cinerary urn. Artists who specialize in this offer many beautiful ones from which to choose. Keep the ashes in a special place in your home. This space should be uncluttered and separate from other things. Place a framed photo of them alongside the cinerary urn. Fresh-cut flowers complete the setting.

Dispensing with the physical remains becomes a sacred task.

Modern times present us with myriad means to honor our loved one's ashes: ceremonies held on a ship at sea where the ashes are given to the ocean; ceremonies where the ashes are mixed in the roots of a sapling that is then planted in a favorite place you can visit the rest of your life; ceremonies on mountain summits where the ashes are carried away in a steadfast wind. Invite only those family and friends closest to your loved one for the dispensing of ashes. Like a funeral, each witness present will want to bid your loved one goodbye with a poem, a memory or two, an expression of love and gratitude for the deceased's role in their life.

Memorials offer a compelling alternative to the old-fashioned funeral. Your loved one's life is celebrated in love and joy by all who were touched by their presence here in life. The gathering can be as small as one other person or large enough to accommodate everyone who wants to participate, whatever this number is. These uplifting ceremonies unite our hearts in love. The best memorials remind us not just that we are all connected to the larger community, but also that your loved one mattered to this wider circle.

Individual participation takes many forms of sharing with the larger group: a favorite memory, a cherished picture, the time your loved one's kindness or generosity touched someone or changed a life. It can be as simple as a poem or your loved one's favorite song. Ask all participants to write their contributions down and collect them in a memorial book or memorial web page.

This will be a treasure.

Be certain to invite love and joy to the celebration.

If the gathering is large, you may want to hold a smaller version of a memorial with your family and closest friends. The only rule here is to not exclude anyone who wants to attend in love. The main event will be a circle of memories.

This is simple and poignant. Form a circle and take turns, going from one person to the next and allowing each person to share their favorite memory of your loved one. Hold hands, embrace, cry, maybe eat and drink too much. And please to God, let some of these memories be laced with humor.

Nothing about this gathering says that it must be a onetime event. During the time ahead, ask your family and friends to join you on the anniversary of your loved one's passing, or better yet, their birthday. You might also include shorter family memorials at holiday gatherings or those times when you become overwhelmed with missing them.

As the future of your grief unfolds, in those times when you feel overwhelmed with missing them, hold a private act of remembrance. Select a favorite outside place in nature: your backyard, a favorite walking trail, or the ocean's edge. Using as many flowers as you like, create a giant heart with the flowers, write the word "love," your loved one's name, or any other symbol of your loved one.

This simple meditation piece connects you to their love. You will experience this gift as you reflect on your favorite memories, the things both large and small that you admired, appreciated, and loved about them, and how very grateful you are for their presence in your life. Be sure to leave tears over the whole. Take a picture as a keepsake.

You will discover how memories shift and change with the passage of time; the small and the meaningless slip away, while love and appreciation grow.

DISPENSING WITH A LOVED ONE'S POSSESSIONS

The material things that belonged to your loved one are treasurable. Whether you place great value on material wealth or are fairly unattached to most things, your loved one's possessions, those that now belong to you, fall into a different category.

At first you discover you cannot part with anything that belonged to them. Just the thought of separating from their things is unbearable; it is as if you are losing your loved one all over again. Sometimes dispensing with their possessions feels like a final goodbye. This creates the idea that you are facing an impossible task.

So, you cling to their possessions as if your loved one is in these things. You might even maintain a whole room full of their belongings and keep it just so in their memory. You find comfort touching, holding, and being surrounded by the physical things that belonged to them.

This is fine. This is normal. Cling to them as long as you need too.

In time, you will realize your loved one is not in their things, any more than you are in your things. How does this happen? When you discover that the emotional connection to your loved one is a by-product of your thoughts and consciousness, rather than the proximity to things.

You will discover there are much better means of connecting to your loved one.

Here is one possibility: Take a favorite picture of your loved one and frame it. Hang it in a place your gaze often lands. Every time you see it, reflect on something you love about them.

This simple practice is common in many cultures. It will surprise you with its potency. You will discover that it forges a stronger link to your loved one than a whole room full of their things.

For, after all, possessions are material things—nothing more.

Eventually you will come to see that your loved one no longer needs a room; they're not there anymore. You will come to understand that dispensing with your loved one's possessions is not a final goodbye. Things only hold the value we assign to them.

Nothing physical is permanent; all things come to an end. Not one thing you own will belong to you in a hundred years; precious few will even exist a hundred years from now. Ultimately, no material possession has any value; the treasures of the Louvre will one day be stardust.

When you feel ready to begin dispensing with their things:

◊ From the collection of their wealth, whether it is a whole house full of things or just a few items, separate anything you feel is a token of their love or representative or reflective of who they are. These gifts of remembrance fall into categories: things sentimental to your loved one or to you; a thing that is symbolic of your loved one's unique character; items they kept close and touched often; something that triggers a happy memory of your love.

◊ Choose one, two, or three of these items as keepsakes. Do not necessarily go with the most valuable. Trust your intuition to make the right selection for you.

◊ Once you choose, invite other people, family members and friends, to select items from your loved one's possessions that are meaningful to them. Surprise yourself with how big your generosity can be.

◊ If any of your loved one's possessions can serve another, it is lovely to gift it to a person or charity. Give away as much as you can (always). Keep practicing your new-found generosity.

◊ Joy is always returned twofold.

If you discover there are things that you don't need and can't use, but still find it difficult to part with them, ask yourself why. If precious memories are associated with a particular item, write these down or take a photo of the item. Make a collage from the pictures, illuminate them in a book of memories, or simply store them in the treasured bank of your consciousness.

Then let the physical item go.

Imagine your loved one applauding this effort.

Imagine your loved one thanking you for doing a good job.

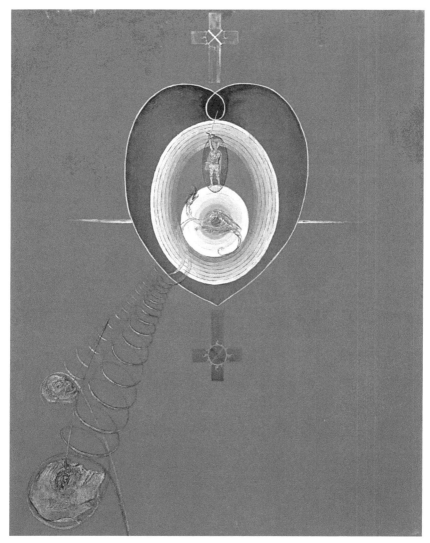

Free Will

IF YOUR LOSS INVOLVES THESE THINGS

If You Lost Your Loved One After a Prolonged Illness

In this age of medical miracles, many people lose loved ones after witnessing their arduous and difficult struggle with a prolonged illness. This passage is fraught with pitfalls. While caring for your loved one through an illness to their passing becomes a sacred journey, the difficulties and struggle change the shape and duration of your grief in surprising ways.

Anticipating the passing of a loved one is to experience that loss—or it is so close as to be indistinguishable. In this way, your grief began with news of the illness and continued for the duration of their struggle. It kept you in a heightened state of alarm and delivered a steady drip of adrenaline and other stress hormones. This has already wreaked emotional and physical havoc on you: sleeplessness, fatigue, indecisiveness, eating disorders—either eating and drinking too much or too little—sometimes irritation, anger, and always anxiety. Be mindful of this.

Perhaps the sun occasionally burst through the clouds during this time; there came sudden hope and the emotional rollercoaster slowed down and sometimes even stopped for a period of time, only to have that hope snatched away again.

Intermittent stressors cause more damage than sudden trauma.

During this time, you were dangled on the edge of a steep precipice waiting to fall. Suspended over this great uncertainty, you witnessed the person you love struggle and endure great discomfort and pain. Often each new day only brought more and greater agony.

When an approaching death has been clouded by pain and suffering, there is only one normal response when it is at last over: relief. Not just the normal relief, but a knock-you-to-your-knees kind of relief. The person you love is no longer suffering. Their pain is gone. Your loved one is free. You are free. The intensity of this relief upon your loved one's passing can be crazy powerful.

Relief *and even joy* can be the most honest and natural part of grief.

Please read that sentence again.

The force of your relief is in no way a reflection of your love.

Rather it measures the difficulty of the passage you and your loved one just exited.

It is important now to make a conscious effort to let go of memories of your loved one's struggle, of their pain and suffering. This tends to happen naturally over time, but there is no reason to wait and many reasons not to, especially if you are troubled by recurring images, thoughts, and memories of your loved one's suffering.

Whenever an unpleasant memory emerges in your mind's eye, do this simple exercise: Stop whatever you are doing and pause. Draw five deep and slow breaths—this alerts your consciousness to a meaningful shift in thinking. Then, simply replace the painful memories with happy memories of the time when your loved one was healthy and vibrant—full of life. Travel down a sunlit path made of your favorite memories until you feel the emotional resonance—the vibration—of these memories.

Employing this memory replacement produces a miracle.

Finally separated from your loved one's struggle, your love begins to intensify.

IF YOUR LOSS CHANGED YOUR SENSE OF SELF

Your life was so entwined with your loved one as to be one. Many or even most thoughts included your loved one. Even the things you did independently were done with your loved one's presence—if not foremost in mind, then nearby—and this is especially true for those who have lost their lifelong partner and we parents who have lost a child. Your loved one's absence is everywhere you look.

You do not know who you are without them. You cannot imagine the self without your loved one, much less a future without them. This ignites intense feelings of helplessness; of being a small, rudderless boat lost upon a vast sea with no oars with which to navigate.

Here's what you cannot see yet as grief continues to flow into the absence writ so large and all consuming: Your loss will change you at your core. Eventually, rather than seeing a diminished self, grief will grow you in unexpected ways. This different person is already emerging as you encounter the new world, day by day, month after month, and year after year. One day you will discover the most meaningful and essential *you* that is still very much here, only . . . more so. Grief is gifting you a previously unknown depth of knowing, understanding, and sympathy, and this expansive intelligence serves as an elixir to a new sense of self.

There will come a time when mirrors will astonish you; you will be looking at a changed self. The sails will have dropped, a strong wind will have filled them, and you will find yourself flying over the waters to a new horizon.

WHEN A CHILD SHARES YOUR GRIEF

Grief in childhood is also a sacred passage.

Like adults, each child's experience of a loved one's departure is unique. The emotional ramifications and repercussions depend less on the child's age and more on how close the child is to the deceased. How they experience their loved one's departure shapes their future understanding of love and its loss. Few things are more important.

The very young child's cognitive abilities are ill-suited to comprehend death and the loss of a loved one. You must help them. Using plain and simple language, share the truth of what has happened. The vital word is *truth*. You may omit any detail or aspect of your loved one's death that the child would find troubling or difficult to grasp, but do not tell a falsehood.

Think of truth as sacrosanct. Truth to human consciousness is as water is to life—absolutely necessary in order to thrive. Lies are the opposite, even with young children—maybe especially for young children. The purpose of lies is to conceal truth.

Here is an unalterable, universal truth: Good cannot come from lies.

One of many reasons is that, on the most meaningful level, human beings recognize lies. Often, without full awareness, when confronted with a lie our consciousness is forced to engage in cognitive calisthenics: What truth does the lie conceal? Do we pretend to believe the lie? What purpose is served by concealing this truth? All of this leads to an unsettled sense of something amiss: Lies cause confusion, distrust, uncertainty, and unease.

This is especially true for young people. The young child's consciousness is self-centered (in the extreme). Most children view the world through the prism of self; everything is about them. Children often create nightmarish scenarios to explain the lies their parents present to them, and more often than not, they assign blame to themselves or to something they did. This is a common phenomenon when a child loses a sibling or a parent. So, it is imperative to tell children the truth about the death of a loved one, and again, in the most plain and simple language possible.

Then make the loss of your loved one all about love. Express your love for the deceased and how very much you will miss them. Most children, bewildered by what has happened, will attempt to comfort you. Hold the child close and let them. Tell them that their comfort is helping you. Thank them.

Express the departed's love for the child. Do this over and over. Tell the child how much they were loved by the one who has passed. Include three memories that illustrate the departed's love for the child. Add details to these memories over time, turning them into treasured stories.

If you hold a belief in transcendence or have a religious ideation of heaven, or even if you are an atheist or agnostic, share with the child the common belief of heaven. Children have their whole lives to work out the ontological reality of heaven, but right now it is okay to let them dream about this healing place where families are reunited in love. They need the comfort and cushion that thinking about heaven provides. Just the story of heaven helps them mediate this loss. Atheists and agnostics sometimes struggle with a presentation of heaven to their children, but you can eliminate any qualms by using these words: "Many people believe that when we die, we go to heaven. Heaven is described as a wonderful place where someday we will all be together again . . . I love this idea. Imagine someday we will all be together again. . . ."

Heaven takes away a child's fear of loss.

A child's grief is different from yours. Expect this from the vast majority of children of all ages, but especially the young child. They absorb the information of their loved one's death and its emotional content, and within a shockingly short time, they behave as if nothing much happened. Even though it can take years to understand their loss, many children appear to return to normal life almost instantly. This sometimes alarms parents, especially parents of teenagers. They imagine their child is somehow unfeeling. But wait. . . .

Something will happen that stands in (substitutes) for the loss and triggers tears of grief. A normally happy-go-lucky child will suddenly become inconsolable over a lost toy; a minor glitch will be catastrophized with a tantrum and tears; a nightmare becomes a traumatic event. You need to be there to comfort the child.

Once the emotions reduce to a simmer, share with them what you like to do when you feel sad ("I like to remember the time when . . .") and review memories of your loved one, especially happy memories that center on the departed's relationship with the child. Poetic sojourns into the past have the awesome power to convey all the love the departed had for the child, and this is what helps the child feel comforted by their memories. Populate these memories with positive affirmations from the loved one ("They love you so much! You know they always thought you were the smartest person since Einstein . . ." and so on.)

Grieving children of all ages—from preschoolers to teenagers—often develop secret fears surrounding how their loss will affect their future. The most common of these is that something will happen to the surviving family members—as if once this door to grief and loss has been opened, it cannot be closed again. You can alleviate these fears with a willingness to discuss their feelings and fears, all the while holding them extra close. Inquire as to their evolving thoughts and feelings: When do you miss your mom the most? Do you ever dream of your brother? Do you ever feel your dad's presence? These conversations should continue throughout life.

It is important to express your belief in the grieving child's resiliency.

For young and older children alike, it is meaningful to create a memorial book or web page of pictures of the loved one, especially pictures that include the child. You can make a sequential book of the deceased's life, beginning at their birth and traveling onward. Encourage older children to turn their fondest memories into written narratives. This can become a book. Add every positive statement of love you remember from the departed to the child. These treasure books can last the child's entire life.

As time goes on, continue to keep your loved one's memory alive for the child. Periodically share stories drawn from their life whenever an external signal reminds you or a memory emerges in your consciousness. Sing prayers in your loved one's name. Play their favorite music when you share favorite moments. Light a candle next to your loved one's picture during birthdays and holidays. Celebrate their memory throughout life.

When grief becomes a bridge to love, this love lights the child's way throughout life. The experience teaches them that their loved one's life mattered, and therefore, their schoolmate's life is important, the neighbor counts, their own life is meaningful. They will have earned a deep understanding of love and loss, and this serves as a foundation their whole life.

Righting the Wrong Turns

Svanen

The light that falls over grieving people is strong and bright; it will always guide us home, but while walking with grief, we can take wrong turns. A wrong turn is one that causes or increases our pain and makes our passage more difficult. These dark passages actually keep us from our loved one and from understanding the depth of our loss; they become our obstacles. Sometimes we need to head in the wrong direction for a while, if only to have the contrast seared into our consciousness when, at last, we turn back toward the light.

Here then are the most common wrong turns.

Anxiety, Worries, and Fear

Multiple anxieties and worries ride in on grief's waves. These troubled thoughts take specific forms that emerge from your individual circumstances. They can loom as large as an IMAX-screen monster and be as persistent as an aching tooth. They can also be embarrassingly petty, where the focus of your attention zooms in on an utterly inconsequential matter, and this fixation, when set alongside the magnitude of your loss, is startling and yet, there it is. Sometimes anxiety arrives in a more undefined shape; you feel a web of generalized disquietude and nervousness.

The most common fears that arise after loss are familiar to us.

Losing a loved one often triggers a fear of loneliness. Your loved one was such a large and essential part of your life; you regard their absence as a void that no one and nothing else can fill. The future appears as an empty and barren landscape. You fear you will never feel love again.

You are afraid you will always be sad and filled with a longing for someone who is not there. The very word *hell* is this unanswered desire. You think you will always be a broken person.

If the loss of your loved one changes your financial picture, you now have worries about money. This can happen even if the loss results in greater financial resources or the dispensing of an inheritance. Sometimes these financial anxieties center on having to perform the tasks that your loved one always did for the household—you worry that you won't be able to figure it out.

Like an invasive vine that climbs and covers a centurion oak, worries and anxieties block the sunlight you need. They separate you from everything good: the love arriving to help you, future joy, and present healing. They can destroy the ancient tree that is the gift of your love.

These worries and anxieties are born in fear. They spring from an imagined future, but one that has not arrived. Fears are make-believe. They are not real.

Fear is always a choice. You are choosing to imagine a bleak future. You are choosing to anticipate this doom.

To demonstrate just how fear works, imagine a child who was told every day that something terrible was going to happen to them, if not today, then soon. We instantly see how harmful this assertion would be, but we also get the trick of it—while it is not true, the belief would begin to shape the child's reality in destructive ways. The child would be inhibited, stunted, frightened. The world the child experienced would be very much changed.

Your fear works in the same way. The purpose of fear is to get more of itself, to grow more fear. This is what fear does. In our material realm, fear works to separate us from love and joy. It is always a wrong turn.

How do you stop? How do you get rid of worries, anxieties, and fear?

By letting them go. When a worry or anxiety or fear pops in your mind, instead of focusing on it and allowing it to grow in detail, visualize the worry as a puff of smoke. Imagine the puff of smoke carried away in a fine, strong wind. The religious amongst us think of this fine strong wind as the Holy Spirit. You let it go.

Then, you choose a different future and imagine that.

Your future is not predetermined. Our country's future is not predetermined. The world's future is not predetermined.

You make choices moment by moment. There is always a low choice and a high choice; each choice brings different consequences, but by choosing high, we begin to create a *better* future.

In this way, the future, *your future,* is always a choice.

You can choose any future you want. You can create any future you desire.

And this is not actually as hard as you may think.

This truth applies to the uncertainty we face collectively. Instead of anticipating a future doom, imagine a great good emerging from this time in history; imagine change as a movement toward equality, a stronger commitment and investment in our children, education, and the environment.

Like all worthwhile things, it takes only the intention and then practice. Set the intention to transform worry and anxiety. The universe answers all intentions, one way or another. This means you will soon find yourself lost in a maze of some worry, but now it will startle you; you will know that the worry is not real. You release it . . . you let it go.

The worry becomes smoke that is carried away.

Now, picture your loved one smiling at you as this happens.

Imagine them promising you everything is going to be okay.

The Answer to Guilt

We often get mixed up about this word *guilt*. Many people consider guilt in a near mythological positive light. Guilt is the feeling that we could have been better. Mother Teresa, the Pope, the Dalai Lama—indeed, Jesus himself—experienced this feeling. To own a consciousness is to know you could have done better, that you are called upon to do better, be better.

This is not the guilt that rides on the waves of grief's emotions.

The guilt that rides the waves of our grief is a pernicious distortion of our emotions. It is the most common and malignant feeling that follows grief. It is always a wrong turn.

The guilt that arrives with the passing of a loved one often becomes a larger psychic burden than our loss. Parents who have lost a beloved child are particularly susceptible to it, and even more so for those of us who have lost our loved one to suicide or violence.

In the throes of our grief, we begin playing the *"if only"* game. We review our loved one's life, mining it for incidents where if only we had done this or not done that, there would have been a different outcome. Our loved one would still be alive.

If only I had steered him to get help sooner, he might still be here. If only I had not let her drive that night, she might still be alive. . . .

Here, we are attempting to rewrite history; we desperately seek another, different outcome—one where our loved one is still alive. Yet we lose this game every time we play it. There is no different ending. These real or imagined things that trigger your guilt do not matter now. There is no alternative ending; your guilt does not change anything.

Guilt serves only to hurt you.

Read that sentence again, and consider:

Even if you do have some culpability in a loved one's passing, and these feelings are always grotesque exaggerations painted by fear, you are already paying the highest price possible. You do not need to hurt yourself more.

How do you transcend guilt? How do you stop this feeling?

By letting it go. Can it be that simple? *Yes*, it can.

Again, imagine your guilt as smoke being carried away by a good strong wind. Refuse, absolutely, to play the *"if only"* game. You might always wish you were dealt a different card, but you weren't. The past cannot be rewritten.

Experience the unalterable truth of these words: Your loved one is gone. This and this alone is what matters.

Because, you see, once you let go of guilt, you find acceptance. Once you find acceptance, you have stepped into the light. You are left with the only thing that matters.

You are left with their love.

A Red Enemy

Anger often emerges in grief. It too, is always a wrong turn.

The purpose of anger (nefarious and no good) is to keep you from experiencing your loss. As we experience rage, we are taken from our loss, its meaning and profundity. Anger is both proficient and devious at doing this. It is a chilling adversary to your grief.

The targets of our fury are anyone or anything viewed as culpable in our loss. Sometimes it is our loved one themselves. For some it is the disease that took our loved one. Others blame another person's actions. God is often the target of anger.

There is always an irrationality to anger. Think of the most extreme example: *A person caused the death of your loved one.* This person already bears the consequences of their action for the rest of their lives. This is the most severe punishment possible. Your anger, strong as it may be, does not affect them; it cannot compete with the fact that they caused your loss.

And if, tragically, there is no remorse here, if this person does not feel anything for having caused your loss, then, my god, you are looking at a damaged person. Damaged people lead damaged, pain-filled lives. Your anger still does not touch them.

Sometimes, when anger shows up in grief, it is because your grief is still too big to know. Experientially, anger might first appear as a fair trade: Instead of experiencing your loss, you feel anger. This is a temporary illusion. Your grief is still there, waiting for your anger to shift, subside, or diminish. It is not going anywhere, no matter how much of the poison you drink.

Some of us feel anger, but aware of its irrationality, we suppress it. We bury it inside. Throughout time people describe this kind of anger with the apt metaphor of a festering wound, one that continuously secretes poison into your body. It still works to keep you from experiencing your loss, all the while growing in ferocity until it manifests in a more harmful way.

Anger only hurts you, its host. It hurts you physically, emotionally, spiritually.

How do you get rid of it?

Acknowledge its existence. Understand its irrationality and how it is hurting you. Then let it go.

Initiate this simple practice three times a day:

Close your eyes. Take ten deep, slow breaths. Now, conjure your loved one in your mind's eye. Relive three of your happiest memories of your loved one in detail. Relive these memories until you experience the profundity of your loss.

Anger holds no presence alongside the loss of your love.

The Mending

One of the most basic understandings that thoughtful humans develop is that we are all so deeply flawed. Our relationships—even with those with whom we are closest, or those with whom we should be closest—are often fraught with difficulties. These troubles can be major life shapers. Sometimes they pull the best of us into a swirling cesspool of never-ending drama and separate us from love and joy, and from each other.

Losing a loved one in these circumstances brings these struggles into sharp focus.

When a loved one passes in the midst of a stormy relationship, or before we were able to reconcile and reach peace in the relationship, the turbulence takes center stage. This can shape your grief and amplify feelings of loss and regret. Not only did you lose an important person in your life, but you feel as if you need to get through a portal that has now been shut.

You start banging on this door with unanswered questions. Why didn't you love me? Why did you hurt me? How could you? Anger at the deceased is a cloak that conceals your pain.

Sometimes this is reversed, and you are overwhelmed with remorse. Why did I do that? How could I have said that? Why didn't I tell them I love them?

(It is a near universal experience: when you lose someone you love; you wish you had expressed this love more frequently when they were alive. The simplest and yet the most profound statement,

"I love you," is so often withheld during life, but so deeply felt in death. You can erase this regret only by learning its lesson.)

You are not just grieving your loved one's departure; you are mourning the loss of the loving relationship that should have been. That could have been. If only. . . .

They should have loved you more or better or differently. Then, you could have loved them more or better or differently. Anger and remorse serve only to bind you to pain.

There is only one answer to this emotional angst. You must find *forgiveness*. Forgiveness is one of the most potent spiritual tools; forgiveness becomes a mighty agent of change. It has the awesome power to transform regret into acceptance and then anger into love.

Forgiveness does not mean you absolve anyone of their crimes or misdeeds, of any injustice perpetrated against you or others. Nor does forgiveness mean forgetting. Forgiveness comes from a much deeper place—it comes from understanding.

Your loved one's inability to love you more or better or differently has nothing to do with you, but rather everything to do with a troubled history woven into their lives. This past, whatever it was, directed them to make unfortunate choices. These choices hurt you and probably other people as well.

Of course, you wish it were different.

Forgiving means only that you recognize this truth.

It can go deeper, still. While we might always wish they had loved us better or more or differently, once you realize their failures of love were driven by the story of their lives, anger disappears. Sympathy beckons. Compassion follows.

Let it in. Mourn the loss of what might have been. Not just for you, but for them as well. While they do not have the chance to choose differently—to right a wrong and grow in love—they are gifting this to you. It is the means of liberating you from a troubled past. You are being given the ability to transcend what has happened.

Forgiveness in grief becomes the most profound gift.

It allows you to step into the light.

IF YOUR LOVED ONE WAS STOLEN BY SUICIDE

Losing your loved one to suicide ignites an all-consuming fire of a terrible angst: anger, guilt, and sometimes shame, all mix into grief, creating an unbearable vortex of pain. Even though you understand that these feelings are wrong turns—that they serve only to hurt you more—because of the sheer *enormity* of all you are experiencing, you need more help.

So right now, I am taking your hand and placing it over my heart.

Listen. Your loved one is begging this of you now. You need to understand why suicide happens to good people.

The answer is presented here as an exercise in imagination:

We are imagining the energetic form of love is the light. We are all born of the one light. You, your loved one, every person on earth is born of the one light. No one is ever outside the light. Our physical form—these bodies—are but temporary vessels for our consciousness, allowing us to experience this . . . the material plane on earth.

As we march through our time here, we inevitably encounter things that alter our light. Picture these as strands of dark energy. This shadow energy brings us fear, anger, shame, hatred, despair, depression, and loneliness. Shadow energy is that which separates us from the light.

Most of us find practices that transmute, push out, and eliminate this shadow energy. These are universal among people and cultures: spiritual, meditative, and religious practices that connect us to love and transcendence; exercise that ignites our sense of well-being; joyful and contemplative activities like immersing oneself in the bounty and beauty of nature, art, and music . . . even elevated thoughts, positivity, and laughter: these all serve to dispense shadow energy.

People end their lives (and do things to hurt other people) when the darkness temporarily overcomes their light. Sometimes this darkness is a small and petty thing that would have, if given the chance, dispersed in a day or two, understood as utterly inconsequential and easily overcome. Other times, the darkness that weighed upon our loved one's light was potent, tenacious, and utterly unbearable. You might know the reasons for your loved one's suicide, or you might never know.

In the most meaningful sense, the reasons do not matter now.

You need only to understand your loved one is in the light now.

All their pain and sadness are gone, swept away like a nightmare upon waking.

Close your eyes. Picture your loved one as their best self. This is who they are now. Only they recognize the burden their suicide has left you. This is what they desperately wish to undo. Because, you see, of their love for you.

Right now, as you read these words, the light of their love for you—so much more than you can know—is shining over you.

Let it in. Hold it close.

Imagine them telling you they are okay now.

Imagine them showering you with a glittering white light of love.

WHAT IS FOREVER

Altarpiece, No. 1

WHAT IS FOREVER

Why does grief knock so hard?

To show you how big your love is.

You discover it is startling, the consuming power of your love. Love is amplified in grief and this amplification is revelatory.

Put your grief, to work. Let it bust open your heart even wider.

Find a quiet time and a peaceful place. Close your eyes.

Take a deep breath, hold for a slow count of three before slowly releasing. Do this conscious breathing for ten minutes, and during each retention, invite yourself to relax. This simple exercise has countless physical benefits: It lowers blood pressure and stress levels, aids your immune system, and shoots positive endorphins into your system. For our purpose, again it serves to alert your consciousness that you are about to wake up.

After the breath exercise, conjure your loved one in your mind's eye. See them smiling back at you. Imagine your loved one is sending you love. Picture this love as a glittering white light cascading over you.

Linger here until this becomes fully imagined.

Invite memories of your time together. Start with the time you felt the most love from them. When was it? Where were you? What was happening as you felt the wealth of their love pouring over you?

Relive this memory in detail.

Remember the first time you laid eyes on them, the very first time you saw them. The moment you first knew you were in love. Think of your favorite anniversary or birthday. Relive the time you both doubled over with laughter. The last time you both stood in awe of a beautiful vista, swam in the sea, or were reduced to joyful tears.

Progress through the treasures of your time together sequentially or let your consciousness choose the order in which your memories appear. Stay here until your eyes are wet with tears.

Picture their love as a glittering white light falling over you.

Do you see now? Their love . . . it is still here.

MORE MIRACLES

Your grief and its intensity of feelings will continue to beget miracles. The very first hint of this is when your perception of your loved one changes. You discover that your loved one's character flaws and faults begin to fade and eventually disappear altogether.

Next, memories of your loved one are viewed in a changed light.

If you are very lucky, this emergent talent begins to spread. You feel inclined to look past faults in other people. These seem like nothing more than the frayed edge of a petal on a basketball-sized rose—a meaningless speck in a much brighter picture. Grief colors human foibles, and they seem negligible now, sometimes even comical. It is like you are an artist now, a sculptor chiseling away, revealing and celebrating the beautiful form beneath.

Sages refer to this gift as seeing people as God sees them.

Mother Teresa, one of the world's greatest conductors of love, had this gift.

Once, it is said, our heroine and Irish singer-songwriter Bono were standing in a line of starving people at a refugee center. Bono said to Mother Teresa, "When I see this long line of starving people, I see an indictment of the human race."

Mother Teresa was surprised by this. "When I look into the face of a starving person," she said, "I see the face of Jesus."

If we could only extend our love and compassion to everyone, how different the world would be! Imagine you saw your loved one in the next struggling person you met. How might your response to this person change?

This is a powerful practice, especially for those of us walking with grief. We are all weathered from life here on earth, but after our hearts have been cracked open, we begin to see past appearances; we want to soften sharp rebukes, rectify oversights, temper harsh words. We encounter an angry person and instead of reacting in kind, we are more likely to wonder what pain or hurt that anger may be hiding. Selfishness and greed are seen less as a damning fault and more as a tragic emptiness that cannot be filled. Now we look past the weather-beaten shell to the simple *and often profound* gem within.

Where once judgment reigned, sympathy takes its place.

Small matters disappear; it becomes impossible to attend to petty concerns. The things that loom large in other people's minds—the relentless push of weeds in a garden, the car that requires new tires, the poor service here, that regrettable situation there— now elicit a small sense of wonder. You sometimes want to take people by the shoulders and ask: Do you know how lucky you are that this is your big problem?

This is what happens when your heart is smashed wide open in grief. Everything appears in a soft focus.

As if to compensate you for your passage, the simplest pleasures are deeply felt, too: a frosty wind on your face, a child's laughter, the consuming lure of music, a happy gathering of friends. An illumination arises from grasping the impermanence of not just us, but all things. It is not just that we see the good, but it becomes magnified and held close to our hearts. This amplifies life and love and allows you to live big and with wide open arms.

What is meaningful is cherished, and the rest slides away.

When You Feel Ready . . . Maybe Before You Feel Ready

Invite joy and laughter back into your life.

You need this. These life elixirs get swallowed up in our grief. Your sorrow consumes them. Grief amplifies emotion, and this works for both joy and laughter. Joy becomes more poignant and laughter sweeter . . . lasting longer, ringing louder. They are waiting to be discovered again.

It requires a conscious effort. Start simply by setting the intention. Say out loud that you are inviting joy back into your life. Take this concrete and deliberate step knowing that smiling incites joy. Try your best to smile at everyone.

As the story goes, once Mother Teresa was surrounded by reporters. One reporter asked her, "Mother Teresa, if you had one wish, what would it be?" Those watching on TV no doubt sighed, certain they were about to hear a platitude, such as a wish for world peace or an end to starvation and want.

Instead, Mother Teresa said simply, "I wish people would smile at each other more." This was brilliant. Not many of us are in a position to bring about world peace or an end to human suffering, but we can all smile more. This simple act is surprisingly efficacious, too. Smiling releases the happy neurotransmitters—dopamine, endorphins, and serotonin, which act like a magic pill. If a person doesn't smile back—who cares? They probably needed to see your smile even more. It will resonate in their consciousness and serve as an invitation to smile the next time.

Joy—or its close cousin, a sense of wellbeing—follows exercise, especially strenuous exercise. These health benefits work to overcome the physical aspect of grief. Whenever possible, exercise outside in nature: walking, running, swimming. Just being in nature promotes health and wellbeing.

Philosopher Ralph Waldo Emerson famously wrote, "People wish to be settled; only as far as they are unsettled is there any hope for them."

What does this mean? *Now is the time to do something you've always wanted to do, but for this or that reason, you haven't done yet.* You have this one life now; you know how precious it is. Ignore the cost, the inconvenience, even the recklessness. If there is something you've always wanted to do, go for it.

Cherish your family members and good friends. Practice every single day saying *I love you*. Let them know how much you treasure their presence in your life. Throw more dinner parties for them. Too much trouble? Make it a potluck. If you are separated by distance, write letters, send snail mail, surprise them with a phone call. Hold the people you love close.

Perhaps the best way to find joy is by doing a good deed. Take a homebound person's dog for a walk or an elderly person on an outing. Slip concert tickets in a music lover's mailbox. Leave a bouquet of flowers or a batch of cookies on a neighbor's doorstep. Plant a tree in a public space—even make it your new hobby, planting trees in your neighborhood. There are a million ways to practice kindness. Find at least one every day.

If you can afford it, gift money to someone who is struggling financially—for no other reason than to ease their struggle. Do it anonymously. Let their joy upon receiving this gift wash over you in force.

Drop twenty-dollar bills in a homeless person's cup. Do they "deserve" it? Perhaps not. Do it anyway.

Volunteering with a worthwhile charity is one of the biggest positive life changes a person can make; charitable efforts resonate with joy. The vast majority of volunteers happily report that their efforts resulted in receiving far more than they gave. Google local charities and as you go down this long list, see what sparks an interest. There are many purposes in life, but one of the most important is to walk each other home.

Add laughter to your life, even if you don't feel like it; *especially* if you don't feel like it.

Everyone can do this: Grab a family member or friend and stare at each other while "fake" laughing. Time how long before it turns into honest-to-God, side-splitting hilarity for real. Catch a live comedy show or watch a favorite comedian on your streaming service. People have cured diseases with laughter; there are more health benefits to laughter than running a marathon. Again, you need this now.

Some lucky people are already immersed in the arts. They enjoy music events, literature, theater, and the visual arts. Even if you rarely visit this meaningful aspect of life, now—with this monumental change—you will find that art experiences are interesting, often cathartic, and always worthwhile. It is easy to do. Every community has various art events open to the public, even if it is often streamed: music events, art museums, poetry readings, theater . . . and you can join a neighborhood book club. Even local high schools put on plays that are often delightful. Art is one of the best ways by which joy, laughter, and meaning return to life.

Inviting art, joy, and laughter back into your life lifts the weight of your grief and helps shapeshift it. These all serve as a reminder that you still have a life to live. Your loved one enthusiastically applauds these efforts.

In the process, you begin to see: you are not so broken after all.

Alterpiece, No. 3

If You Choose

Grief will open the doors to the spiritual realm, if you choose.

Religions throughout time have built edifices in an attempt to help people know the spiritual realm, but it is still very much a mystery. The unsettling reality for most of us is that we feel a separation from that which is transcendent; a separation prosaically described as *existing behind the veil.* Some who are steeped in the certitude of a religion grasp the reality of the spiritual realm as truth, but don't often (if ever) experience it. Others have a vague notion of the spiritual realm, but rarely give it any consideration; they think it is a possibility but then conclude no one knows for sure, no one can know for sure. Still others are skeptical of the reality and place the very possibility under a vast umbrella of fantasy.

This covers the wide spectrum of human belief in an afterlife.

You have some understanding of the spiritual realm.

While it is not the purpose or point of this book to dissuade you from your religious and spiritual beliefs, understandings, and proclivities, in order to illuminate the spiritual aspect of your grief, it is helpful to shine a light on the profound mystery of the spiritual realm. This illumination begins with a brief reflection on the astonishing, mind-boggling complexity of life right here on this planet.

This complexity in the material world is everywhere we look. Science, the most powerful tool available to humans, has found no place in the known universe where, upon close inspection, it discovered "hey, look here, this is really simple." Quite the opposite. Everywhere we look we find a staggering intricacy and complexity in form, function, and operation.

Here is a short detour that serves to highlight this point:

Out of trillions of possible examples, let's take a peek at the "lowly" beetle. There are over three hundred thousand different species of beetle, accounting for one of every five species that cover the globe. Evolution has tried, refined, and tested beetles for millions of years and created an amazing creature. They have been used as jewelry, food, art, but more interesting, when scientists begin analyzing beetle physiology, they find brilliantly engineered forms. But first and foremost, they are critical to our biosphere and play an important role in the health of our ecosystem.

Countless innovative inventions have come from studying the beetle. For instance, the *Onaymacris unguicularis*, a beetle found only in the Namibian desert, has a unique way of procuring water. As dew-enriched fog settles over the dunes in the morning, the beetle's shell collects it, which it then slurps up. The Dew Bank Bottle replicates this ingenious design, and literally collects water from the air, which in arid environments could save lives. Another type of beetle's feet—dense pads of tiny hairs—inspired the development of a new reusable and adhesive-free tape that is twice as sticky as other flat tapes. Physicists have also studied the iridescent metallic colors of jewel beetles, which reflect different wavelengths of light to produce an awe-inspiring shimmering effect. Still other scientists are exploring ways the beetle's design genius could prove useful for engineering optical chips in ultrafast computers. The list of beetle- inspired inventions and innovations goes on and on with no end in sight.

All this comes from a partial inspection of just one type of insect.

Again, this complexity is in all things in the material world: there are about three hundred and seventy thousand known species of flowers, representing a riot of brilliant colors and an astonishing variety of form. The microbes inside your intestinal tract number in the trillion,s and each microbe is as complicated as the computations for the gravitational interactions of stars in the galaxy. The mating habits of baboons fill books. A single hectare in the Amazonian rainforest contains more tree species than the whole of North America, an innumerable variety of plants, fungi, and animals, and most of these are still unknown. The entropic miracle of rotting wood in a forest's ecology presents a byzantine complexity of multiple systems operating together.

And then, if we happen to look beyond our beautiful blue dot, our solar system consists of one medium-sized sun, orbited by eight planets, moons, asteroids, comets, and meteoroids, which exists with over a hundred billion other stars and Sagittarius A* (the supermassive black hole inside the Milky Way, which is itself just one of trillions of other galaxies in our universe). Astrophysicists are now pondering the likelihood that our universe is just one in an infinite number of universes. Astronomy is the science of ever-expanding horizons, and these words are a wholly inadequate understatement.

The complexity of the material world is quite beyond the limits of our individual comprehension, and this is worth your contemplation when considering the spiritual realm. Because, quite simply (small pun), the spiritual realm is immeasurably more complex than our material world, for our material world—the whole shebang—exists inside of the spiritual realm. Spiritual teachers tell us that there are *infinite layers* of the spiritual realm, like spectrums of light that go on forever. One can travel up through the spiritual universe, encountering spirit community after spirit community. But, just like heading out in a spaceship to find the edge of the universe, you would never come to an end.

The spiritual realm becomes like a giant ink blot in our imagination; we can see anything in it. This is the mystery. There may be no light to shine on this mystery, except this:

The experience of transcendent hope belongs to all living sentient beings, and it is especially meaningful and poignant for those of us who have lost a loved one. Connecting to your loved one in the spiritual realm is often the most profound, moving, and transformative experience in a lifetime. It will not only change your life, but it can save it—lifting you from a cold and dark and lonely place to stand beneath the bright light of the sun.

Your grief will gift you this, if you want it.

Here's the important point for the skeptics among us: Belief in this reality is not a prerequisite for this to happen, but you do have to want the experience. The experience will fuel your belief and shape it accordingly.

It will be exactly what you need in order to know the energetic power of love and its transcendent reality. While for some, the first connection to spirit arrives with a big wow, what we consider a religious experience more commonly arrives as a soft whisper. Like the signal from a distant radio station, you adjust, tune in, and begin receiving more.

As soon as you set the intention of connecting to your loved one, spirit begins searching for the best way to make this connection for you as an individual. What triggers a response—wonder, excitement, gratitude, or a question mark—determines and shapes future connections.

All that is good in the spiritual realm manifests positively on the material plane; all that is good in the physical realm resonates powerfully in the spiritual realm. The two are mirrors of each other. This is meaningful.

It is why everything that works to connect you to spirit has powerful positive benefits in our material world: meditation practices, prayer, pranayama or breath practices, exercise (especially if the exercise comes in the form of a spiritual practice, like yoga or martial arts), wellbeing practices such as veganism (especially as a by-product of expanded compassion for our fellow creatures), fasting or caloric-restrictive diets (health permitting). This is one of many reasons why developing your connection to spirit becomes a life-enhancing choice.

This cannot be emphasized enough.

The converse is also generally true. Alcohol and drugs restrict consciousness and inhibit your ability to perceive the spiritual, especially in the beginning. To initiate a connection, it will help if you refrain from alcohol and drugs as much as possible.

And understand that love is an energy. Too often our experience of love is narrow and restrictive; we think of it as a box of chocolates or a bouquet of flowers. People even think of love as a feeling or emotion. Love can *cause* feelings and emotions, but it is an energy.

Here is how you initiate the experience:

◊ Return to the earlier loving kindness meditation.

◊ Find a quiet time and a peaceful place. Close your eyes.

◊ Perform the simple breathing exercise.

◊ Conjure your loved one in your mind's eye smiling back at you. Relive your most poignant memories. In detail. Then, once again, imagine your loved one showering you with love.

◊ Picture this love cascading over you as a glittering white light.

◊ Now ask them (out loud or silently) for a confirmation of their continued existence: Can you send me a confirmation that I will recognize as a symbol of your love?

◊ Thank your loved one in advance.

◊ Send the glittering white light cascading back over them. Picture them opening their arms to this visual image of your cascading love. See them laughing or smiling as the glittering white light falls all around them.

Repeat this loving kindness meditation every day, twice a day. This simple meditation practice trains, teaches, and alters your consciousness for the connection that awaits you. The more you practice it, the stronger the connection grows.

Within a month, but often the same day, or the very next day, your request will be answered. You will experience a confirmation. How your confirmation appears varies widely from person to person. The connection is a fantastic dance between your consciousness and your loved one. It can also include the wider spiritual realm that supports you.

At first these signs can be vague and uncertain. Again, spirit is seeking the best way to connect to your consciousness. It is building a velvet bridge to you.

The first signs can be energetic. This means that as you are meditating, or thinking of your loved one, you feel a tantalizing tingling, whisper-soft electric raindrops brushing your skin. Some people experience this in a more pronounced way, even as goosebumps.

The energetic connection can also come as a buzzing sound in your consciousness. Hilariously, this can be very much like tinnitus, with the difference being that a spiritual signal is altogether pleasant; the buzzing is experienced as both external and internal, and it disappears when you shift your consciousness to the external world.

Often it arrives as the energetic form of love washing over you. You feel love as a physical force and as soon as you realize what is happening, it intensifies. It is indescribable how this stream of energetic love ignites your consciousness as it cascades around you. You feel it physically, emotionally, spiritually. This can be so overwhelming as to drop you to your knees and wet your eyes.

You amplify these connections with recognition, gratitude, and excitement. Spirit is looking for your response. This is what forms the initial link to your loved one.

For many others, perhaps most of us, the connection that first appears is synchronistic. You determine if it is a sign from its emotional resonance. These signs also tend to appear when you are thinking about your loved one—or conversely, when you encounter the sign, your consciousness connects it to your loved one. You might at first feel wonder, then bafflement, then wonder again. You are asking: *Is this a sign?* The question is joyful.

In George Bernard Shaw's play *Saint Joan*, it is said, "Imagination is how God speaks to us." This is deep on many levels, (hilarious, if you are an atheist). Spirit uses your imagination to communicate. Even if it is not a sign and just a coincidence, if you take it as a sign, spirit employs this trick of imagination to strengthen the connection to you. The sign will soon be repeated, or you will receive another sign.

Here are the most common signs that begin building this velvet bridge:

> *Music*: Any music that connects you to your loved one and appears unexpectedly in your field. Your loved one's favorite song, a symphony you heard on a memorable anniversary, lyrics that light in your consciousness with new meaning. You can use music to connect to your loved one. Play their favorite song or piece of music, while visiting memories of them. Ask for a connection. The music will often show up in your field in the following days.
>
> *Wild animals:* Birds, circling butterflies, and ladybugs are common first signs. Our loved one's favorite animal. A beautiful fawn standing alone on your front lawn, staring back at you. Whenever something about the encounter with the animal is special or unusual and resonates with mystery, even if it still leaves a question mark.
>
> *Reoccurring symbols or repeating numbers appear in your field:* Beautiful bird feathers in unlikely places . . . a familiar scent . . . the word *love* . . . your loved one's birthday written numerically on the license plate in front of you . . . a series of four-leaf clovers . . . famously, a penny from heaven—with a date that has meaning to your life.
>
> *Dreams:* Your loved one appears in a vivid dream. You know it is a form of communication when it happens; again, it resonates differently than most dreams. The most common

of these dreams is a phone call from your loved one, which symbolizes the desire to communicate with you. Your loved one will build on this.

You will get more than one sign.

You can get a hundred or more signs. Some of us need this many.

Your loved one will use your consciousness to forge the bridge back to you; they are discovering what works. Your loved one wants this connection. It amplifies the light of love. They want to give you the lifesaving affirmation of transcendence. Their transcendence is also yours.

Your loved one desires more than anything for you to experience their love. They want to ease your pain of separation. They want you to know their love is still here . . . that love is forever.

You have only to want it.

Building the Velvet Bridge

Grief always has another chapter.

It will invite you to go deeper because, you see, grief has changed you. You are more sensitive. You are more aware. Grief has expanded your consciousness. You are connected to the spiritual power of love. This gives you the opportunity for a powerful transcendent connection.

Grief will ask you to write the next chapter. The next chapter inevitably leads you to become more of what you are meant to be. The opportunities to do just that arrive because you now understand that life is meaningful, short, and precious; you are meant to make the most of it. You have been called to connect to deeper currents of love, joy, understanding, and service.

You will recognize the invitation when it shows up. These invitations appear in myriad ways: books, classes, art and music, your volunteer work, a new and compelling path presented by a teacher. It sometimes arrives through travel experiences.

These invitations most frequently appear in opportunities to help other people.

If you choose, your loving kindness meditation will help you discover the next chapter in your life.

Begin by enhancing and amplifying the effects of the basic beginning breath practice. Again, breath meditation practices work physically, emotionally, and spiritually, and nothing is simpler to do or more beneficial once practiced. The list of physical benefits of mindful breathing exercises is long: It lowers blood pressure, reduces stress-inducing hormones, increases blood circulation, and triggers relaxation. It also aids in any task performance, especially cognitive tasks.

The spiritual benefits are priceless, but the first gift of the practice is to teach you how to focus and direct your consciousness. The vast majority of us go through each day of our lives as the unwitting passenger to our thought trains. Most of our thoughts are pointless, especially in modern life where we are constantly bombarded with meaningless stimuli, and our thoughts are easily led astray or serve no good purpose. Many thought patterns are actually harmful: worries, anxiety-triggering hypotheticals, and inconsequential musings. Once you learn how to control your consciousness, you become the director of your life.

This is a wonderful and empowering place to be. You don't just learn how to mediate and change your response to the world, but you actually discover how easy it is to alter your reality for the better. Meditation becomes the answer to a multitude of modern challenges.

A breath practice teaches you all this and more. Here are the basics:

◊ Sit upright, unless you're more comfortable lying down. Lying down is not normally recommended for meditation practices because many of us fall asleep when relaxed, but if you feel more comfortable laying down, then simply set the intention of staying awake.
◊ Focus on the sound and feel of your breath. Inhale deeply through the nose, while expanding your breath shoulder to shoulder and down to your abdomen. Exhale slowly, with awareness. Repeat.
◊ Invite yourself to relax on the exhale.
◊ When your thoughts wander—and they will wander— simply return them to your breath.

Like all worthwhile things in life, you build proficiency with practice. Begin with five minutes of conscious breathing and work up to twenty. Practice throughout the day, and especially any time you feel anxiety, worry or fear, or negativity.

As taught earlier and as you become more skilled and comfortable, add a three-second retention on the inhale. Hold your breath for three seconds at the end of the inhale. Now, as you experience the benefits of this, add a retention pause of three seconds at the end of the exhale.

Finally, practice both a retention on the inhale and one on the exhale.

This is a basic pranayama meditation practice.

Now, use this energetic breath to amplify the power of the loving kindness meditation.

At the conclusion of a meditation practice, imagine your loved one in your mind's eye. Picture the glittering white light of your love showering over them. See them with open arms as the light falls all around them.

Relive the memory of your loved one that brings you the greatest joy. Add details. Return to the image of your loved one beneath the light. Fill your heart with this love. The feeling connects you to an energetic form of love, and to your loved one. If you continue to practice the loving kindness meditation, you will eventually reach a point where you do not need memory triggers to connect to energetic love. You will be able to state it as a fact: I am in my love.

Imagine this love as a glittering white light.

Think of a family member. Imagine the glittering white light cascading over this person—like the touch of Tinkerbell's wand (corny, but also visually potent). You can magnify the energy by reliving a happy, loving memory of this person.

Send love as a glittering white light to each of your family members in turn.

Here's an important point: Joy follows love; it always follows love. Imagine the person laughing or opening their arms with joy as the glittering light cascades over them. Stay here as long as the feelings last, as long as you feel the energy.

Let go of any troubling aspect to the personality of the person receiving the cascading white —this is important for the practice. See each person on a soul level, or as their best self.

Now, go through your friends in this same way—seeing them as their best self, as the glittering white light of love spills over and around them. Imagine them laughing as this happens, their arms flung upward in happy exhilaration of the experience.

Next, go through your co-workers, sending each of them love.

Include your neighbors and any other person in your world.

Now, think of someone else you love who is no longer with us: a grandparent, parent, child, or friend—anyone, so long as you love them. Start by visiting your happiest memory of this person. Relive it in detail; when inviting our consciousness to relive a memory, it often becomes quite vivid. Let emotion flood your consciousness. Send the glittering white light cascading over them.

Thank them for being in your life . . . for the gift of their love.

If you experience tears, a tingling sensation, or the buzzing in your ears, this is spirit answering your gift. It is a powerful experience.

No doubt, as you go through the people in your life, someone will pop into your mind whom you find it difficult to send love to—a controlling parent, a quarrelsome teenager, a troublesome neighbor (every neighborhood has at least one), an unpleasant coworker, a prickly and contentious uncle. You will discover your grief softens these feelings. This is a gift. A loving kindness meditation is the most effective tool on earth, and probably in heaven as well, to ease anger and animosity. It is more effective than a year's worth of therapy. Most people naturally tend to focus on how the difficult person affects them, but instead try to imagine them stripped of their trouble, difficulties, personality particulars, and tangles. Instead, picture them as their best self; see them transformed by laughter and love as you shower them with glittering white light.

At first, you might find it hard to send "difficult" people love; you don't *love* them and that's that. If you experience this, just imagine the white light as blessings. Lift them up—they need it. You will be flabbergasted at how this spiritual practice manifests in the material world.

At the end of this meditation, imagine a cascade of love falling over you.

Practice metta-meditation every day—then, twice a day. Metta-meditation is a type of meditation where you connect to the energetic power of love and then use this connection to lift other people. For our purposes, we will first use it to connect to your loved one.

On the material plane, this has amazing benefits. The practice alters your consciousness in a powerful way. You are literally rewiring your brain to give and receive love. Love, the most meaningful experience on the planet, becomes an important aspect of your life.

Within two weeks of practicing a metta-meditation, people begin to respond to you differently. It can be as simple as the warmth of their smile, a lingering touch, or an unexpected intimacy. Words cannot convey how much magic there is in this practice.

Metta-meditation changes you at your core. These changes are everywhere you look. The effect is dramatic.

Do people actually receive the love energetically, or are you somehow changed from the experience? The answer is: Both are true. You are becoming a conductor of love.

Keep in mind, also, that you can practice this anytime, anywhere.

Miracles happen when we open our hearts to the energetic power of love.

You see the divine spark everywhere . . . in everyone and every being.

Next, at the conclusion to your meditation, ask a question or seek help in any area of your life. You are asking your higher consciousness, your loved one and spirit team . . . the light . . . God (contrary to many popular and ancient beliefs, names do not matter).

Ask for a deeper understanding of an issue or for more information. Ask for help with a relationship or a difficult task, for clarification on an important decision. You can request guidance in a particular area—just be as specific as possible. Your specificity helps spirit provide the right answer for you.

Importantly, you can ask for the next step in your spiritual awakening.

Spirit will always answer. Your higher consciousness kicks into greater awareness. You will be directed to the answers you need. There are infinite ways this happens—it is part of the adventure.

This beneficial and powerful practice alters your consciousness over time and expands your understanding and experience of love. Energetic love is boundless—expansive and infinite, like the universe itself. Your higher consciousness starts directing you to better choices. It also makes you aware of negative thoughts and their consequences; you begin eliminating unhelpful thoughts. You become more compassionate, sensitive, kind, and loving, and you open the doors to previously unknown abilities inside yourself.

It strengthens the bridge to your loved one.

Discovering Your Purpose

Grief is a powerful spiritual path once you understand:

◊ You are a transcendent soul. Again, belief doesn't matter here; what resonates as truth in the spiritual realm reverberates as truth on our material plane.

◊ You are aided by your spirit guides—all the souls that love you . . . and there are many more of these than you know— you chose this life for a purpose.

◊ You selected this time to incarnate—in this body, in this exact place. You chose your mom, dad, and siblings. If you have children, you entered a spiritual agreement with them to be their parent. Your higher self selected the pivotal, most important aspects of your life.

◊ You and your loved one chose this incarnation together.

◊ The question now becomes: *Why?* Why did you choose this life?

◊ This vantage point can be an illuminating and life-affirming lens.

◊ You have free will. Your parents had free will. All choices reverberate energetically into our lives. Fate is never predetermined; our choices can result in tragedy or fortuitous circumstances bringing forth joy and love.

◊ Your grief is presenting you with this very choice.

Many spiritualists propose tragic life events happen to test or hopefully ignite our soul's compassion; that tragic situations are not chosen as punishment, but as a powerful spiritual path, with untold benefits in the spiritual realm. You may never know why something happened, and the purpose of your life choice might forever elude you, but we move closer to discovery by asking these questions.

This examination includes you and your loved one.

This is where grief leads you.

Imagine you had not made this choice: You had never met your loved one. Your loved one never showed up in your life. You never knew their love. You never felt their touch or kiss, you never heard their voice or laughter. The treasure bank of your memories together—gone, swept away as if they never happened.

Can you imagine this? Do you see the tragedy here?

Now what if you were given this choice: to have known their love and its grief, or to never have known this treasure.

Your imagination is introducing you to grief's biggest gift—gratitude.

Let it wash over you in reflection. Let it change the shape and size of your grief forever. The understanding it brings is the most beautiful part of love and its loss. It is your loved one's gift to you.

The magnitude of your loss becomes the size of their gift.

Grief is indeed a teacher bearing gifts. To have walked in love is to come at last to this final great sorrow—it can be no other way. Yet grief is also our doorway into an altered world. Compassion, letting go, forgiveness of yourself and others, and grace—all wait on the other side of this door. These incalculable gifts lead to a knowing of transcendence. Grief, then, becomes the brightest light on your soul's path.

A path lit by love—your loved one's love . . . shining in your heart, mind, and soul forever more.

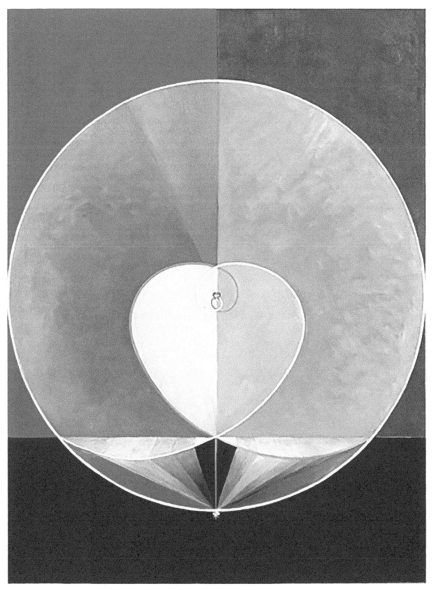

The Dove, No. 13

About the Author

JJ FLOWERS is a screenwriter, the creator of a number of children's books, including the award-winning *Juan Pablo and the Butterflies* (under the name of Jennifer Horsman), and the author of several historical romances. She has also written *The Spiritual and Scientific Power of Veganism*. When not reading and writing, JJ Flowers enjoys spending time with her beloved family, friends, and pets, teaching yoga, and healing walks.

ABOUT THE PUBLISHER

LANTERN PUBLISHING & MEDIA was founded in 2020 to follow and expand on the legacy of Lantern Books—a publishing company started in 1999 on the principles of living with a greater depth and commitment to the preservation of the natural world. Like its predecessor, Lantern Publishing & Media produces books on animal advocacy, veganism, religion, social justice, and psychology and family therapy. Lantern is dedicated to printing in the United States on recycled paper and saving resources in our day-to-day operations. Our titles are also available as ebooks and audiobooks.

To catch up on Lantern's publishing program, visit us at www.lanternpm.org.

facebook.com/lanternpm
instagram.com/lanternpm
twitter.com/lanternpm